GROW FROM YOUR PAIN

A HEART-RENDING STORY OF A TEENAGE GIRL

MANISHA KALLEM

To the orphans,

may you all lead a life with a lot of courage and determination.

To all girls,

help yourself in overcoming any painful circumstances.

And to my parents, my brother and my friends.

Contents

Preface

This book has taken birth from a true story, of me as an orphan from a tender age. It describes the problems and pain that I had gone through and my process of struggle in overcoming those as a teenage girl. I started writing this book when I was 16 years old. And I am at the end of my teenage years when I am getting this book published. The story mentions all the major incidents in my life starting from when I was 12 years old to 19. It will help the readers learn how to treat their pain so that they can gain a profound value from the process.

Books allow our souls to reside on the earth even after our death.

1

Getting close to my teenage life drew me to a point where I started thinking about my past life, sitting on the edge of a cliff on a cool evening, remembering the days that I had spent with my mother and father. Those were happy-go-lucky days but unfortunately didn't last long. Where a happy life is everyone's goal, as an orphan, making myself well-built was my only dream and that would fulfil the word "HAPPINESS" in my life. I often tried to inject a new quality into my personality from the ordeals in my past. Thinking about all this stuff, I started walking back home. As I reached home, I tried to take a nap as my brain was exhausted from my overthinking. I tried to pen down all those things in my diary, but in just a few seconds, my inner soul said, "Following our thoughts and converting them into actions is much more better than making up notes."

I convinced myself to take a nap for some time; I closed all the curtains and lay down on the cot, trying to lock my blinking eyes. Suddenly, I noticed a narrow beam of sunlight coming from somewhere through a tiny hole in the window, falling straight on my left eye. In a moment, that beam lightened my brain and a few lines crept into my head...

The darkest room can reveal the importance of even the narrowest beam. That made me realise that a small beam can stimulate our brain to generate numerous ideas and a small opportunity can push us bigger. This beam reverted me to a thinking state again and my sleep vanished with my neural stimulation. I sat with some deep loneliness in the evening breeze, remembering a day when a 12-year-old me, standing in front of our house, giving an untainted look at the crowd, in a complete dilemma about the state of the environment around me. All eyes around were staring pitifully at me. I was agitating within my mind and heart. There was a sudden, loud and grief-stricken voice from somewhere; my father was calling me, "Mani...!" He was crying his eyes out in deep grief.

Observing the situation, a painful tensity penetrated into my heart. An ambulance arrived, my heartbeat was getting worse, and my eyes found her figure...my mother! My heart was torpified for a few seconds and it caused a sudden jerk in my head. The hope of living my life with her was betrayed at that moment. But the fear of facing the day of her demise had been roving in my brain since the day she had made a suicide attempt.

My life with my family before this had been happier and healthier. I was the merit kid of my parents, grabbed a free seat in Navodaya through an entrance exam when I was in my 5th standard, and I was studying 6th grade in Jawahar Navodaya Vidyalaya. My parents were so proud of me. Everything seemed so normal for me till the day my grandmother came to my school and informed my teachers about my mother's suicide attempt. She told me that my mother had burned herself with kerosene and was hospitalised. My grandmother took me to the hospital, and I was very scared to see her in that state; however, I stepped into the burn-ward in Gandhi Hospital and my eyes caught her lying helpless on the bed and burn wounds all over her body. She was about 90 percent burnt.

My loquacious throat was not able to speak a single word at that moment but my mom found her voice from somewhere and told me to eat well and to take care of my younger brother. I just shook my head and left the room with water in my eyes. The words she spoke were repeatedly oscillating in my head and increased my fear of losing her. All of us had a hope that she will recover but our minds reminded us of the doctor's words that she can't live more than a month. She had already lived 20 days in a state that a girl can't describe. On the 21st day, the doctor, in a low voice, told us that all her organs were severely damaged and suggested taking her home so that our relatives could see her for the last time. Those were excruciatingly painful words that a girl at my age didn't know how to react to.

My father sent me and my brother home with one of our relatives. My mother, father and maternal grandparents decided to come in an ambulance in the early morning. But it seemed that God was not satisfied with my mother's deathly suffering; the ambulance driver's sleepiness made the ambulance fall into a ditch and that day, my mother's situation taught me the meaning of PAIN. All the broken glass of the ambulance had pierced her burn wounds. My father's head was severely injured and our poor grandparents got fractures in their arms. She struggled to even take a breath from early morning to 10 PM that night.

Unknown to all this, my soul was searching for my mother alive in the ambulance. But seeing her corpse made me think how stupid I was to hope that god would recognise her pain and make her well soon. My mother's decision over suicide was not understandable to me at that tender age, but it was told to me that it had happened just because of some quarrel between my mother and father. But I don't think my mother was that stupid to take such impetuous decisions for silly reasons. As days passed, I realised that *a girl's life not only begins when she comes out of her mother's womb but a new self-dependent life can also be embarked upon after her mother's death.* The tender girl in me decided to undertake a new life as a bold woman.

A woman with a phlegmatic mind
Always able to impart peace of mind
Tackles every problem with different versions of her mind
Serves and satisfies, at last pleads everyone, not to mind
Limits her ardour, under the guidance of her mind
Just think from every end of your mind
Before you suppress a woman's mind
Because she has some million things residing in her mind
That she can't even express to humankind

♡♡♡

The thought of self-dependence is not a weakness, it is food for a great challenge in women.

♡♡♡

One day, I woke up after experiencing a bunch of nightmares during the night that disturbed my healthy sleep. I tried to interlink all of my dreams for a while and had a thought that my life had some hidden connection with my dreams. But soon, I left it as a foolish thought and started cycling to my favourite spot as was usual in my routine. As I reached there and sat on the cliff, I noticed a fresh green leaf floating on the water there. The peaceful green colour wriggled into my mind and it taught me something. A leaf that is soon going to drown in a water body, *looks green*...Then, why can't a man with a small failure come up with evergreen ideas...

I suddenly turned around as I felt like someone was calling me; it was my brother standing there, asking me to come home as some of our relatives were waiting for me. It was the day to offer some rituals after a year of our father's demise. I left that place along with my brother. As we reached home, everyone started sobbing, remembering the day my father died, leaving me and my brother as orphans on this earth.

An uncle of mine called me and said, "As the elder one, you should take responsibility for yourself and your brother, you should prove yourself as I heard you are a merit student. Take care, dear!" Those words were scrolling in my mind throughout the day. At the end of the day, almost all the relatives left and it was the time of sunset; I started going to the spot with the diary in my hand. That uncle's words were still living in my mind and I realised that one profound responsibility of mine was to design a beautiful future for my brother—not as a sister but as his mother. I also decided to shower as much love and care on my brother as I would give my son in the future and to shower as much respect on my husband as I would give to my father so that we both can be the parents for my brother. At least then I could expect our lives to go forward as before.

Since I was habituated to penning down all of my decisions in my diary, I opened it to put in the decisions that I had made about recreating my family. I noticed it was not only the day after one year of my father's death but also 6 years since my mother's demise. That day was like facing all the seasons in a single day. If there will be a day like this, any human body might have a chance to fall sick, so I had chosen a busy schedule with my studies as a fruitful remedy for it.

Unfortunately, my remedy stopped fighting for me as situations got bitter after 4 years of my mother's death. Since my mother's death, my father was well concerned about me and my brother. Even though I was growing older day by day, he used to look after me as an infant. He became my whole world, mother, father, best friend...What not! Years passed on, but after 4 years, the days started getting bitter and strange. My remedy was not at all working for me, my busy schedule was completely broken and I didn't even concentrate on my studies as before. The reason for this weird cause in me was unexpectedly my father...

My father was driven by our paternal grandmother to marry another lady. She persuaded him by saying that a mother is obligatory to look after growing children. Fate brought us a stepmother one day. A queer hatred towards my father crept into my heart without my knowing. My brother and I convinced ourselves to accept her as our mother because we thought that she might at least take care of our father. We respected and cared for her as much as we cared for our mother. But that wicked lady suppressed our father physically and mentally. And our father was not at all taking care of us as before.

One day, I returned home for the Dussehra vacation. That lady did not even hand me a morsel of food to eat. Neither did she offer me a glass of water nor did she speak a word with me. My little heart drained out in those unforeseen circumstances. I was ravenous throughout the night. I was dying inside remembering my mother's quest to feed her daughter's empty stomach. Tears flowed down my cheeks and the whole pillow became so wet by morning. My father was helpless and did not say even a single word to the lady. The next morning, observing all the heart-rending incidents, my father, in despondency, thought that I may live my life much better away from home.

He took me to a private hostel in the town. He left me there and he turned to his bike to start the return journey. But my heart couldn't take that anymore. I was crying my eyes out and running along with my father. But he was in an impatient state and left me on that street road. That evening, it was raining heavily. Standing alone in that rain, I felt like I was orphaned from my mother's womb. I was mentally not strong enough to face this mysterious world alone, till that day. But the insight into these experiences made me iron-willed to handle any kind of situation.

I sensed something at that moment. "No one can shape my life; I should escalate my life in the best possible manner." Imagining one of my hands as my father and another one as my mother, I ran towards the hostel with a determination to achieve something worthwhile, sheltering myself from the rain with both of my hands on my head. With eyes full of tears and heart full of determination, boldly consoling me not to cry until the day my father would come back to me after my eminent success in the contemporary world by gaining name and fame as his daughter. That single day brought a lot of courage and confidence in me rather than grief and sadness.

At that time, I thought to ask my grandmother to take me to their home. But my father didn't like me to stay there, so I destroyed the thought in a second. After recess, I called my grandmother and I pleaded with her for some financial assistance to manage the hostel fee there. She told me that she would come and pay the hostel fees the next day. The next morning, she came and paid the fee and gave me some pocket money. But she was continuously asking me to come to their home. I resisted saying 'Yes' and convinced her by saying, "I have some classes here which I should attend daily without fail, so I have to stay in this hostel."

At last, she left the hostel with an eyeful of tears. For about a month, I lived there with a busy schedule even though I would feel lonely at night. I started spending hours and hours in the library. One day, on the way to my hostel room, the hostel warden reminded me to pay the hostel fee for the upcoming month. I explained my situation to her and I requested her to allow me to stay there for at least three more days so that my school will get reopened by that time and I can vacate the hostel and stay there from then on.

Understanding my problem, she allowed me to stay in the hostel for the next three days. I went to my room and when I checked my mobile, there were so many missed calls from my grandmother. I called back and came to know that my father had not been well for the past one week; he was mentally depressed and my stepmother left home about four days back. My mind became heavy after knowing all this. Unexpectedly, that was the day of my 10th board results. I started searching for my results online and found that I had gotten a 10 GPA.

The other side of my mind was too unstable about my father's condition. That day, I made a major decision regarding my intermediate education. I wished to study an integrated course in Psychology in which I had a very keen interest. But thinking of my situation at that time... "Mother is nowhere, Father is not well, my grandmother cannot afford the college fee for my further studies. What to do? Where to study? How to pay the fees?" Those were the questions scrolling in my mind.

There was still a chance to study in the 11th and 12th standards in my school for free, but the stream I wished to pursue was not available in my school. If I convinced myself to pursue any of the courses available in our school, even then there was a question, "Who would support me for my further studies after 12th standard?" Finally, I decided to apply for IIIT Basar, where I could study an integrated 6-year course for free. But I was not at all interested in getting into that since PCM was the only available stream there. But I convinced myself to study there and I pleaded with my grandmother to arrange the school fee for my brother by borrowing from some money lenders.

On the day after my results, I called my brother to ask him about taking our father to a hospital. But I came to know that he had already been admitted to the hospital since he was not well. At that moment, my self-consolation made me pen these lamenting lines.

Lighten the heart to weigh more
Leave the sadness to live more
Hold your happiness to laugh more
Love the people to get back more
Tackle the problems by yourself to achieve more
Face your individual needs, to learn
the deepest lessons for life, more and more...

Just two days were left for me to vacate the hostel, and 4 days left for the last date of application for IIIT. So, I was in a hurry to collect the certificates mandatory for the application. I went to the school where I had studied from class 1 to class 5 for collecting the certificates, then I went to Jawahar Navodaya Vidyalaya to get the certificates from class 6 to class 10 and returned to the hostel at 3 PM. I was too tired because of the long journey on an empty stomach since I didn't have anything from the previous day. I wished to have lunch but lunchtime in the hostel was over. But I was unable to cope with my hunger. I thought of eating outside. But soon, I realised that I only had 50 rupees left with me and I should go to our Mandal revenue office with that amount to get the residence and income certificates. It would cost me exactly 50 rupees to travel there and back. I took my bag and started walking hurriedly towards the bus station because the scheduled time for the bus was 3:30 PM. As I crossed the entrance of the bus station, the bus started leaving the exit gate. I started running and at last, caught the leaving bus.

I reached the MRO office at 4:30 PM and I came to know that it might take more than a week to get those certificates. But I was worried and approached the MRO. Luckily, he said that he already knew me and he appreciated me for my 10th marks as he had seen in the newspaper and helped me out in getting the certificates soon and he stated that a merit student's life shouldn't be ruined because of some certificate delay.

After submitting the applications for all the required certificates from the revenue office, I returned to my hostel with a bloated empty stomach at 10 PM. Again, the hostel mess was already closed. I just lay down on my bed as soon as I entered my room.

The next day, I woke up to the call of our hostel owner. She told me that this was the last day for me to stay in the hostel and that I needed to pay the fee if I wanted to stay back.

I couldn't call my poor grandmother again for the fee and didn't want to put her into trouble for every struggle that I faced. At last, I decided to vacate the hostel and go back to our school so that I could stay there without any second thought of fees and all. Because Navodaya Vidyalaya was such a heaven for me which had fed me for 5 years and was still getting free education and food. But my only fear was, "Where should I study after completing my intermediate at the school?"

I knew that fear would be overcome if I were to get a free seat for a 6-year integrated BTech course in IIIT. The classes for the 11th standard were already ongoing in our school, and I was attending those on one side and waiting for IIIT admission results on the other side. My mind was tensed from day to day. At last, one fine morning, I heard the news that I was shortlisted for admission to IIIT through my 10th percentage along with the NCC and state-level chess certificates that I had earned.

Unexpected happiness at that moment, but no presence of my dearest parents to share the moment.

I ran to our housemaster in the school to share the news. She was the one who looked after me as a mother throughout my school life. Hearing the news, she pulled me closer and congratulated me with a gentle hug. The very next person who felt very happy about this was my grandmother. I called her and informed about the admission and requested her to take me to their home because our school wouldn't allow us to leave without an escort. By evening, she came and took me to their home.

Still, there was no full-fledged satisfaction in me about the news as shortlisted students might also lose their seats in the counselling. Anyways, my grandmother and I started the journey to attend counselling on the scheduled day at the university. After reaching there, a notice at the entrance gate made me feel nervous because it was stated that the university will select 1 student out of every 3 who have been shortlisted. Security there sent us to a waiting room where we should stay until I will be called.

After 20 minutes of stressful stay in that room, they called me inside the cabin. A madam sitting in the centre of the panel team was verifying all of my certificates then she said that I could leave. But when I turned to leave, she suddenly asked me to stay back and asked for my NCC certificate. She couldn't find that in the file I had submitted. I was worried that I hadn't received that certificate from the school. Then I requested the panel team to give me half an hour for submission. I immediately contacted my NCC master to ask about this. He said that our school can provide a provisional certificate for students in case of any urgency until the original certificate will be issued by the head office. He asked me to apply for a provisional certificate as per the procedure to be followed.

But there was no time left for me to go and apply for that because the journey from university to our school itself would take half a day. But I had been given only half an hour. I luckily had the facility of sending an online application through WhatsApp. Our NCC master took a lot of responsibility for helping me out in that situation; he took the printout of the application and got it signed by our principal. But that application needed to be submitted to the battalion in Karimnagar. I requested one uncle of mine who lived in Karimnagar to take that signed application from the school and submit it to the battalion. It nearly took one hour for my uncle to do all this. Finally, he submitted the application to the battalion but he called me and said that it might take 2-3 hours to issue a provisional certificate because the chief was in a meeting at the collector's office.

My tension got multiplied. I and my uncle requested the people in the office a lot but they said that they couldn't do any favours since the chief's signature was a must on the certificate. Meanwhile, I approached the counsellor madam to explain my situation and to request an hour more. She declared that only half an hour was left to close the whole counselling session. She also informed us that there was an hour more until the results were disclosed. Half an hour passed, and all the students were requested to move for lunch.

But I decided not to have lunch until I had submitted my certificate as my stomach was already filled with anxiety. 10 minutes after the announcement of lunch, I heard that the chief had returned to the battalion for lunch. Luckily, I received a soft copy of my certificate after a lot of struggle. I ran towards the counselling room to submit it, but it had already been locked.

That moment made me depressed and desperate. I felt like I had lost all my energy in one go. But still, without losing hope, I ran to security to know the address of the staff room. He directed me towards a room on the first floor. Luckily, I found the counsellor madam there. She noticed me and I showed her the soft copy of the certificate without any delay. She asked me to take the print of that certificate and submit it to the academic section.

Experienced a moment when a single piece of paper decided my future...

When I handed over that paper to the academic section, for the first time, I felt like my empty hand was filled with a handful of satisfaction. And my tension-filled stomach started feeling empty as I felt relieved after the continuous struggle.

Grandmother and I were waiting for the result...The time arrived and my struggle succeeded, the panel team was announcing the finalists on the stage, and I was one...

I felt so relieved at that moment, it was like I got charged directly from 0 to 100. And then, there was a way for me to step on. That moment framed the lines below:

A successful crop can bring happiness to a farmer
A super hit movie can bring happiness to an actor
A gifted child can bring happiness to their parents
A free seat in a University can also bring vast happiness to an enthusiastic but financially backward student

Even though that was a happy moment for my state of mind, there was a guilty feeling of missing my father's happy face. There was no visible possibility for me to even share that news with him. I joined IIIT three days post the counselling and was accommodated in an allotted hostel room.

I was busy transforming my way of life by making new friends and building a very good knowledge base. Two months made their way into the past and finally, a day came when my father was getting discharged from the hospital. I was so excited to see him but surprisingly, my father made a phone call to me and said that he will be coming to see me. A poem took birth from me to express that eyeful excitement to see him while I was waiting for my father at the main gate of the University.

Dad, when Mom left this world
Half of my heart was dead
But I made my hope as a sword
And You and brother as my only world
Then I started working hard
To prove my mom's word
When this world made you sick
I made my decisions much thick
I tried not to lose hope, all over the clock
And I kept myself up to the mark
I awaited your visit
on every other parent's visit
My tears convinced me to allow them out
But I restricted my eyes in letting them out
Because I know there will be a day
when you visit me and say
that you missed me every single day

On that day, my father took me home for the Dussehra vacation but unfortunately, my stepmother also visited home the same day. She was hiding her intense jealousy with excess love. I kept observing her extreme caring towards my father. But I was having some melancholy about the sudden change in her behaviour. She was extremely melodramatic. One day, she blurted out that she was wishing for my father's death in front of me and my brother. My father didn't know about that and we didn't even tell him about the incident with a view of not making it big. Seeing me crying, my father understood that something was not quite right there and he didn't want me to get hurt by her anymore.

The next day, he told my brother to drop me at my aunt's house. After the festival, I returned to the hostel. But after a week, when I was sitting in my class and about to get a lunch break in 10 minutes, my mobile started vibrating and I noticed that my cousin was calling me continuously. She also sent me a message: *Please take the call, it's urgent!* and that worsened my heartbeat. I was waiting for the lecturer to leave the class but I was very worried and I stood up and requested him to allow me to go out. And when I called back my cousin, the news that I heard was the second major heartbreak in my entire life. My father had made his way to heaven and left me and my brother alone to face this world. He had committed suicide by taking an insecticide.

Deep grief in my heart
No mortal to escort
Neither a creature to control my soul
Nor a benefactor to steer my goal
My right gave me the conviction
My left controlled my emotion
Eyes became proactive for future
The heart became provident to nurture
A little girl's emotion
On the day of her mother's cremation
A little girl's emotion
On the day of her father's cremation

You are the only one who can rescue yourself from any kind of pain.

ღღღ

3

On the third day of my father's demise, I was thinking of moving back to college for my exams which were to start the next day. Every one of my relatives asked me to stay back for some more days until I had become stable and were convincing me that it was okay to skip exams one time. Those words were completely contradictory to what I was thinking. I believed "Stability wouldn't come as time passed, it should come from our thought process."

I answered them, "It's the quality of a strong daughter to stop nowhere to make their parents feel proud. Skipping these exams causes months of delay in my career which ultimately delays the event which brings name and fame to my parents. And I need to go!"

I returned to college on that day, I started living with their memories and I was not at all worried about my life but the guilt lies in being a daughter and I didn't get a chance to at least spend a single penny of my earnings on them to make them feel proud. About ten days after my father's demise, I came to know that there was a huge amount of bank loan to be paid, which had been taken by my father. My tiny brain had no idea as to how to manage that huge payment. I was perplexed and stuck in my thought process.

Mind: High goals to achieve.

Heart: No support to receive.

Mind: Huge loans to be paid.

Heart: No money in hand.

Mind: Are you looking for some care?

Heart: Yes! But I was left alone somewhere.

Mind: Why are you sitting in the noon sun? I am going off with this scorching heat.

Heart: I am already off into pieces. My dear eyes, please let me leave my pain out.

Tears started flowing down my cheeks and surprisingly, they were answering the questions in my mind.

Tears: Dear Mind, are you worried about your goals?

Mind: Yes, but how can you help me?

Tears: When I step out of the eye, I always travel downwards due to gravity... But if you can stop me from coming out by fighting against gravity, then it gives you the strength to start your journey.

Mind: When people are not at all showing some concern and taking every chance to suppress me, reminds me that I am alone. Then I am not even able to control you at that moment.

Tears: Okay, when people suppress you with their words or actions, let me out for some time but remember! Each time I come out, you should add a new goal to your goal set. That goal should mesmerise the one who has suppressed you.

Mind: How can I manage financially?

Tears: You should buy a vehicle called confidence which will automatically drive you to the solution. But remember that vehicle can't move without any input like hard work.

Mind: But, how can I console the heart; it is too emotional and feelings-oriented.

Tears: Dear heart, please make yourself a rock until the day when your success makes me come out as two single drops from the eyes followed by a broad smile. Those two drops are your mother and father who are celebrating your success together. That should be the day to exert your emotions back on this world.

Heart: Thank you, tears, you have taught me the reality. I will remain a rock until the clock points towards success.

Tears: It was really a great time with you all...Bye guys! See you on the day of your success.

Mind: Until that day, stay safe inside and don't try to step out. This is pandemic time, coronavirus is planning a world tour. Lol!

My determination taught me a fruitful lesson:

When we eat a banana, we throw off the complete peel as waste.

When we eat an apple, we throw off the peduncles and also the seeds which contain harmful chemicals like cyanide.

Similarly, if we want to achieve a goal, there are a lot of things around to be cleared out of our way to our goal and to make an ideal fruit named success which can be eaten directly without any leftovers.

When it was already a month since my father's demise and the repayment of his loan was still pending, officials from the bank were frequently calling me to clear the loan within a period of 10 days. They warned me about seizing the land kept as surety on the failure of repayment of the loan. I was in college at that time and needed to give my examination the very next day.

I called my maternal grandparents to explain the issue to them without asking for any money and I waited for their reply in the hope of receiving some word about financial support from their side. But I didn't receive one. I didn't even ask them for any help directly, keeping their financial status in mind and not wanting to impose on them anymore.

I got an idea to sell a piece of land to manage the loan and pay the fee for my brother's education. But that was a big deal which was difficult to handle within the span of 10 days and with my exams on top of me. One of my relatives suggested writing a letter to the bank explaining the situation and requesting them to provide some cut-off amount to be paid within 10 days rather than the whole amount and allowing us to pay the remaining amount within 3-4 months.

As I needed to go to our regional bank for the same, I was waiting for my exams to get over. After giving my last exam of intermediate, just 3 days left of the time given by the bank. I packed everything from the hostel and was about to board the bus when I realised I didn't have any money even for the traveling charges. I ran back to the hostel and requested some money from one of my friends. She gave me a bit more than what I had asked for and I promised her that I would return that soon. That was my first request with no guarantee of the number of days that I might take to return that money, which made me use the word 'soon'.

But I knew I would definitely return that amount to her one day. Traveling for about 5 hours and just an hour more to reach the bank, it was already closing time. So I decided to get off the bus at my village's stop which was on the same route so that I could stay there for the night and approach the bank in the morning. I went to my home, which was just a house and not a home for me anymore. It was a late night with dim lights and dusky rooms. Everything felt empty there, I wanted some soothing touch of my parents on my stressed head, wanted some food prepared by my mother for my hungry stomach, and wanted their presence to express all my pain. But I decided not to cry. I started compensating for my expectations by feeling the things that they had left for me. Feeling a soothing touch by touching their photo frames. The pleasure of having delicious food made by my mother by moving my arms gently over the kitchen shelves. Finally, feeling their presence by writing into the diaries they had gifted me to extinguish my pain.

I went to sleep with a hungry stomach by consoling myself and understanding the reality. The next morning, I straight away went to the bank. It was around 9 AM and all the bank officials were arriving and setting up everything. I approached the help desk and I asked them for an appointment with the bank's manager to submit a request letter. They asked me to wait for some time so that they will arrange a meeting according to the manager's schedule after he arrived. Hours passed and finally, after 4 hours, they asked me to go in and I went inside the manager's cabin.

I explained my complete financial and family condition and requested him to provide a cut-off amount to be paid and asking for some more time for the remaining amount. He was a very humble-hearted person and he spoke to some higher authorities immediately regarding the issue. Luckily, they also accepted the request and asked me to pay the quarter amount of the loan in 2-3 days and the remaining amount within the upcoming 3 months. I thanked him and promised that I would adhere to the conditions given. I was so happy moving out of the bank but within seconds, I realised that I had to arrange a quarter amount of the loan to be paid in 2-3 days and I didn't have even a single penny in my hand at that moment.

Hold your emotion
Start your mission
Just hide the tears
Start the actual gears
There should be a day
Where this track gets reversed
All the gears at their destination
Indicating the accomplished mission
Hidden tears into success carriers
With an outburst over emotional barriers

I returned home and noticed our land tenant waiting for me to discuss the annual amount to be paid to us. I asked him for a tentative date by which he can pay the amount and I was thinking to ask him to pay that amount in advance to repay the loan in the bank. He answered that he used to pay the amount in the June of every year and he also asked me about the loan issue as he had heard that from somewhere. I explained all the things and also requested the advance payment. He agreed and told that he would arrange the money within 2 days. He gave the money as he said and I paid off the quarter of the loan amount in the bank.

I started thinking of some solution to make our financial status stable until my graduation so that I could earn post that. As I had thought of selling a portion of land previously, I met a well-known person in our village who was experienced and good at dealing with such type of land sales. He explained to me some complex issues that we had to sell that land. About 5 years ago, my father had sold a piece of land just beside the land that I wanted to sell at the moment. The actual problem was with the survey numbers of those two portions of land which got interchanged when my father did the registration to the buyer.

The person who told me all this was the same person who had dealt with our land sale in the past. If I wanted to sell that land, I need to approach Mandal Revenue Office for the clearance of the issue before making any commitments. The very next day, I approached the tahsildar's office to discuss the land issue and the process for the clearance. After waiting for hours and hours, I was told to come the next day to meet the officer. I returned home and came back to the office the next day. I decided to meet the officer on that day and I kept requesting the worker there to allow me into the meeting room.

At last, one of my father's friends who works there in some role noticed me in the office. He called me and asked me about my presence there. He expressed his condolences to my father and he also took me to the tahsildar for the meeting. After analysing the issue, the tahsildar advised me to approach a lawyer to file a request in the District Revenue Office. I called my maternal grandparents for a contact number of any known lawyer. I got the mobile number of a lawyer and contacting him, I was told to meet him at his office in our district. I went there, I filed a request with his help and I submitted that to the District Revenue Office.

A few days passed, and my lawyer called and asked me to check the updates by approaching the Mandal office as some response from the district office was sent to them.

I approached the Mandal Revenue office again and I came to know, as it was stated in the response letter from the district office, that if the previous buyer of the land agrees to the exchange of survey numbers then we could make the clearance immediately. But once I approached the buyer for informing the same, I came to know that he was afraid to make this exchange because of the petition sent by our maternal grandmother from the court on behalf of us to register the complete land in our names after my mother's demise. He was not sure whether he would get the land legally post the exchange of survey numbers.

I approached our lawyer to ask for some help in this. He again explained a process for the same. A few weeks passed, and my schedule only had courts, revenue offices and lawyers those weeks but still, everything remained unsolved. Meanwhile, my intermediate results were declared. Hell yeah! My obtained marks were the same as the total marks. Those results answered the questions of my relatives behind my move to college on the third day of my father's demise to give the exams.

Free your brain by making a success from your pain.

Those were the days when I was looking to take a major step in my career, that is, choosing a university for my graduation. I could not afford to pay any more fees for my studies, so I decided to grab admission from a good university that would also offer me a full scholarship. I already had an option of staying back in IIIT which offered me graduation with no cost. But there was a lack of specialisation in AI and ML in Computer Science Engineering which was my area of interest. So, I started searching for universities on Google. Exploring and comparing many of them, I decided to join Bennett University which also agreed to provide me with a 100% merit-based scholarship for the tuition fee. Everything seemed somewhat better then.

Since that was Covid time, our university scheduled tentative online classes for our first semester. I needed to move to the city since we had no proper network in our village for me to attend the classes online. I and my brother had thought to rent a room in the city so that he could travel to his college easily and we had a good internet connection there so that I could also attend classes effortlessly.

We executed as we had planned. I somehow managed to cook food for months and schedule the washing of clothes and cleaning of the room. Even doing all that work every day while attending classes hadn't stopped me from doing something extra in parallel. I started tutoring two of the children in our area so that I could pay off the room rent with that amount.

Tutoring two of the children in the street
Felt great respect in their greet
Sacrificing one hour of my day
Taught me the importance of a holiday
Evoking new thoughts in the tiny minds
Made me recall my childhood times
Raising my voice to make them understand
Realised the struggle behind my teachers' sound
Being a tutor as an orphan
Brought back all of my unforeseen fun

After a very short span of that serene environment, I fell down the stairs of the building where we were living. My back and legs got injured to an extent that I was not in a state to even walk without some support. Since I was unable to cook food and do things for myself, my maternal grandmother came to stay in our room until I got well. The next day, I woke up early in the morning to attend the scheduled classes on that day. My grandma was already up. She told me to sleep for some more time and to skip the first class as I was sick.

I answered her, "Grandma! Sometime later in my future, if someone asks me why my scores are less in a particular academic year, I don't want to narrate to them the stories about every small health problem to make an excuse."

She felt very happy with what I had said. On the same night, my grandma filled water into a new bottle without noticing the silica gel packet in it. After waking up, I unknowingly drank that water since the bottle was just beside me. I haven't even noticed the colour of water in that sleepy state. After some time, when I was about to drink water again, I noticed the colour of the water and I remembered that it was a new bottle. I asked my grandmother if she had removed the silica gel packet in it.

She said that she hadn't noticed any kind of packet in it. It was then confirmed that I should see a doctor. We went to the hospital that night itself and doctors made me try to vomit out forcibly. They gave me multiple injections and tablets. About 3-4 hours later, my body started dehydrating even after taking in a lot of water. Doctors prescribed some medication for that but still, the dehydration continued. Even before getting well from the previous injuries, the new one continued to oppress my body for a week. On one hand, I was trying to come out of my illness, and on the other hand, I got a phone call from the bank to remind me that there was just one week left to pay off the remaining loan.

My brain froze for some moments. Then I started searching for people in my contacts list who could help me financially at that moment. My eyes went to the contact of my physics sir in my previous college, which reminded me of his words when I was leaving the college—to ping him for any kind of help in the future even if it was any financial problem and not to hesitate for contacting him. I immediately texted him for help. Within 24 hours, he transferred the money to my bank account without any agreement or any kind of surety. That really brought water to my eyes. I strongly decided to give double that amount to sir in return on the day I would receive my first salary.

I cleared the complete loan with that amount and my brain got freed about 1 percent for 1 minute. The reason behind the "1" thing was that I started expecting problems and filling my brain completely with complex premonitions beforehand, so whenever any of my problems got solved, I would enjoy them for 1 minute by filling that free space with a new premonition. So whenever I actually faced that problem, it seemed like a routine for me. Everything at this moment might showcase a negative vibe but in practice, that will lead to a very positive life. Yes, I just hope for the best but I always expect the worst.

Balancing your heart and brain:

If your heart weighs more than your brain
Discard the relationships causing you strain
Rescue your heart from the huge drain
Add a skill to your brain which makes it gain
If your brain weighs more than your heart
Add some ethics to your life chart
Try to bring meaning to your spirit
Which undoubtedly makes you love it

As months passed, my second semester came to an end. No further instructions from our university about the classes offline. My brother and I had moved to separate hostels in the city. Just after joining the hostel, I was unpacking my luggage and I noticed my phone was vibrating somewhere inside the bag—it was my brother's call. A piece of news that could replace a premonition in my brain made its way into my ears after answering the call. My brother informed me that he had taken our paternal grandmother to the hospital as she was not well but unfortunately, she was diagnosed with symptoms of kidney failure. He had already spent all the money we had for the tests and doctors advised us to admit her there immediately.

My brother asked me to come to the hospital but it was already late at night and I couldn't find an auto on the road. My brother called me again and said in a hurry that we needed to pay 10 thousand rupees more in the morning, if she was not discharged by midnight. That was around 11:30

PM and only half an hour left for us to decide.

Meanwhile, I found an auto and I reached the hospital. The scene that I saw after getting down from the auto was another major heartbreak and my eyes couldn't hold back the tears. My brother was in a severely injured state. His legs, shoulders and fingers were covered with bandages with blood stains on them and he was still pushing the stretcher of my grandmother towards the exit. I ran to him and urged him to answer what had happened to him.

He then told me that he had met with an accident which he hid from me intentionally because he didn't want to worry me. I once again approached the doctor requesting to allow us to stay there for that single night. But he didn't agree. I started calling my relatives for some help in finances or some manual support as both of them were suffering. No one answered the call even after calling multiple times as it was late at night. But that situation reminded me of the absence of my parents for the first time after their expiry.

My brother took treatment in a government hospital for his fractures to save money for our grandmother's treatment. Both of us had shifted our grandma to the government hospital that night. They started all the procedures by 2 AM. The hospital was very sparsely occupied as it was midnight. I took our grandma to the second floor of the hospital where she needed to be admitted and I asked my brother to stay back downstairs as he looked so tired while walking with those injuries. I set all the things for her there and told her that I would be back within half an hour to get my brother to eat something as he might not have had any food since morning.

While I was walking down the stairs, I noticed an unknown man walking behind me at speed and making some uncomfortable sounds. I was afraid and increased my speed of walking as he was almost near me. As the situation worsened, I started running down the stairs and finally saw my brother in front. The tense vessels of my heart were relieved. Being a girl, it was not safe to move alone even during our toughest times in this cruel world. A question in my mind at that time was, "if I would have had my father with me at this moment!"

I searched everywhere around for food stalls to get some food for my brother, but everything was closed that night except a paan shop where I bought just a water bottle for him. That was the best I could give him at that time. I made him have some water and we rested our heads on each other's shoulders, sitting in the hospital ward until sunrise.

The next morning, I had to give my internal assessment test but I was roaming around the medical shops and tiffin shops around the hospital. I gave my test on the mobile by walking on the footpath and carrying breakfast in one hand. The reason I hadn't skipped a single test was that I was trying my level best to retain the scholarship offered by our university for the next academic year where I should score above 80% in the current academic year. At around 10 AM, we consulted the doctor. He advised us to take her home with the given medication until we decided on a kidney transplant.

We took her home and I stayed there for a week until she was able to walk and eat by herself. Then I returned to the city since I needed to start giving my final exams the next day. I reached the hostel and had a satisfactory sleep after two weeks. I woke up in the morning about 40 minutes before the exam. I freshened up and was trying to turn on my laptop when I had only 15 minutes left for the exam. The laptop was not starting at all. I tried connecting and disconnecting the charger. I tried holding the power button for long. But nothing worked. I ran to an internet cafe nearby and finally started my exam 20 minutes late.

Post the exam, I took my laptop to a service centre. They told me that the laptop's motherboard needed to be replaced and might take about 10 days. I had my exams exactly within those ten days. I called some of my friends to borrow a laptop from one of them. One of my friends told me to come to their home town to stay there and give the exams from their home because she had some work with the laptop within that period. I gave my exams there and I came back to the hostel after finishing my last exam.

A few months passed, then I was in my 3rd semester. One morning, my brother called and told me that he had been suffering from fever from the past 2 days. I advised him to go for a check-up in the hospital. I thought it was some normal seasonal fever. But again, it was not. He was diagnosed with dengue which is very commonly diagnosed nowadays. But the doctor warned that the high severity of the infection had affected his platelets count to an extent where he might get into a comatose state. I immediately asked him to get admitted to the hospital and I started my journey to Hyderabad where the hospital was located.

Once I reached there, the doctor told me that it cost about 10,000 rupees per day if he got admitted to the hospital. I didn't have enough money to pay the bill even for one day. But without any second thought, I first told them to confirm the admission. I tried multiple ways to arrange money for his treatment. On one side, his platelet count was falling extremely low and I was the only one there to take care of him. I was roaming around the blood banks for donors, leaving him alone in the hospital.

On the other side, I didn't have enough money to buy medicines for him. My close friend's father helped me a lot by lending us a huge amount for the treatment. My tension about finances got relieved but my brother's condition was raising my heartbeat. Even after multiple platelet transfusions, his condition was getting worse. I was trying my best by feeding him with the required nutrients from various foods. I didn't sleep for 4-5 consecutive nights being vigilant about his condition. My body also stopped bearing the sufferance. It caused me nausea and vomiting. I became so weak because I haven't had enough food for a week. My migraine and cluster headaches were irritating me too much. I was also on my periods and I was unable to even walk to the nearby medical store for medicine for my brother due to the abdominal pain. What was left to increase my pain?

My 3rd semester's final exams also started online. I used to give my exams with a stressful mind and a dreadful heart. The thing was, I scored full marks in the very first exam I gave in that situation. And that was the toughest subject for all of my friends. Whenever I suffered from more pain then I have determined to give my best performance. That was the only strategy that drove me forward in my life in any kind of circumstances.

My brother completely recovered in a month after a lot of struggle. I felt the absence of my parents during those tough times but I tried to make my brother feel their presence from me.

If I observed my life over the past 4 years, I recognised a pattern in the problems that I was facing. I used to get external problems such as financial issues, brother's and grandmother's health problems, etc. in all the 18 months of every 2 years and when I struggled to escape from those,

I used to get a span of 6 months where I again suffered from internal health problems. People might think that observing such a pattern brought nothing to me. But that pattern taught me to be prepared for any kind of problem, over all 365 days, every year, whether an external or internal problem.

As a teenage girl, I had many wishes to enjoy my life with my parents as my friends do. Sometimes, I wanted to ask my mother to cook my favourite dish, ask my father to buy a mobile phone for me, and go home for vacation. But every wish of mine was like a dream in the reality. I was habituated to searching hostels during every vacation, accustomed to the hostel's food and the environment full of friends who became my family.

My stressful mind with numerous thoughts used to generate a lot of nightmares in a fast-forward manner which caused me shortness of breath every single night for months. I had spent a number of sleepless nights, being seated in my bed, due to those horrible nightmares. I decided to visit a doctor many a time but I delayed it every time due to lack of money. But I stopped nowhere in my career. Finally, I saw the doctor with the first stipend I earned from one of my internships. I started fulfilling my deficits with my own efforts. Build a new skill in yourself for every new problem which can help you improve your skillset too.

Everyone has their own problems and pain. Overcome your pain by comparing yourself with the people who are facing more problems than you. If you are reading this, you can compare and feel the pain of the people who can't even read. If you are able to see these letters, you can compare and feel the pain of the people who can't even see. Every pain has a super pain for it. If you try to find that out, then your pain seems so smaller for you.

ღღღ

Gain something from your every pain.

ღღღ

9 798887 491523

Printed by Libri Plureos GmbH in Hamburg,
Germany